ANCIENT CHINA

BRIAN WILLIAMS

Viking

Acknowledgments

The publishers would like to thank the following for permission to reproduce photographs in the book:

e.t. archive: pages 4, 7, 11, 12, 17, 19, 21, 22, 23 (top left), 29, 35 (bottom right), 36 (left), 39 (bottom), 40, 43 (bottom right). **Zefa:** 14. **Michael Holford:** 15. **The Bridgeman Art Library:** 18 (left); Giraudon/Bibliotheque Nationale, Paris, 18 (top right); British Library, London, 23 (bottom left); Oriental Museum, Durham University, England, 34–35, 35 (top); British Library, London, 39 (top); Bibliotheque Nationale, Paris, 46–47, private collection. **Werner Forman Archive:** 23 (center right), 26 (bottom). **Christie's Images:** 26 (center left), 43 (top). **Science & Society Picture Library:** 30. **Bodleian Library,** Oxford, England: 31 (MS. Bodl. 264. Fol. 218R top). **Fotomas Index:** 36 (right). **Wellcome Institute Library,** London: 37. **Ashmolean Museum,** Oxford, England: 42 (1978.1836). **Reverend Karrach:** 44 (left). **Robert Harding Picture Library:** 44 (right), 45, Mark Stephenson.

Illustrators
James Field: cover, 10–11, 20–21, 26–27
Mark Stacey: 6–7, 14–15, 16–17, 28–29, 38–39
Peter Bull: maps, 4–5, 30–31, 44–45
Bill Donohoe: 8–9, 24–25, 32–33, 40–41
Simon Williams: 6–7, 12–13, 16–17, 18–19, 22–23, 30–31, 34–35, 36–37, 42–43.

VIKING
Published by the Penguin Group
Penguin Books USA Inc., 375 Hudson Street, New York, New York, 10014, U.S.A.
Penguin Books Ltd, 27 Wrights Lane, London W8 5TZ, England
Penguin Books Australia Ltd, Ringwood, Victoria, Australia
Penguin Books Canada Ltd, 10 Alcorn Avenue, Toronto, Ontario, Canada M4V 3B2
Penguin Books (N.Z.) Ltd, 182-190 Wairau Road, Auckland 10, New Zealand

Penguin Books Ltd. Registered Offices: Harmondsworth, Middlesex, England

First published in Great Britain by Heinemann Children's Reference,
a division of Reed Educational and Professional Publishing Ltd., 1996
First published in the United States of America by Viking,
a division of Penguin Books USA Inc., 1996

1 3 5 7 9 10 8 6 4 2

Copyright © Reed Educational and Professional Publishing, Ltd., 1996

All rights reserved

Library of Congress Catalog Card Number: 96-60284

ISBN 0-670-87157-5

Printed in Belgium

CONTENTS

China's unique civilization developed over thousands of years. Each period in its imperial history, from the Shang dynasty to the Manchu, produced great achievements in art, philosophy, science, and technology. China today is a powerful modern state, building on the triumphs of the past.

Kingdoms and Dynasties

500,000 years ago: cave dwellers

25,000 years ago: Stone Age tool makers

3000 B.C.: Yangshao and Longshan farmers

1700 B.C.: Shang kingdom

1122 B.C.: Zhou ruler overthrows Shang king

500 B.C.: Confucius

221 B.C.: Qin dynasty—First emperor, Shi Huang-di—Great Wall

202 B.C.: Han dynasty

A.D. 220: Period of unrest—Buddhism

581: Sui dynasty

618: Tang dynasty

907: Civil wars

960: Song dynasty

1279: Mongols rule all China

1368: Ming dynasty

1644: Manchu Qing dynasty

1912: Chinese Republic

1949: China becomes a Communist state

Today more than a billion people in China share a unique history. Theirs is the world's oldest continuous civilization, a culture that has lasted for more than 5,000 years. The Chinese believed their country was at the center of the world. When a regional prince sought independence in A.D. **960**, the Chinese emperor asked in bewilderment, "What wrong have your people done, to be excluded from the empire?"

PREHISTORIC CHINA

From excavations of their camp sites, we know that the first Chinese lived in caves more than 500,000 years ago. Remains of these people, known as Peking (Beijing) Man, were found in the 1920s at Zhoukoudian in northeast China. They lived by hunting, fishing, and gathering food, made stone tools, and probably used fire.

Much later, about 25,000 years ago, more advanced cave dwellers made polished shell ornaments. They buried their dead with some kind of religious ceremony, sprinkling the bodies with red dust.

THE FIRST FARMERS

The heart of ancient China was the valley of the Huang He, or Yellow River. The river takes its name from the yellow soil washed down in its waters from the high plains of Mongolia to the north. This yellow soil, known as loess, was

A bronze cooking pot on three legs. It had a lid, and stood in the fire for efficient cooking. It was made in Shang China between the 16th and 11th centuries B.C. Decorated vessels like this were cast in molds. A clay impression was taken from a wax model. The clay mold had several pieces that interlocked like a jigsaw puzzle to produce the finished vessel.

also blown by the wind and covered much of north China.

In the fertile soil of the Yellow River valley, people began to grow crops and live in villages. This was about 5,000 years ago, and it marked the beginnings of a settled Chinese society. The early village communities were led by chiefs, who were probably priests as well as warriors. From these leaders emerged China's first kings, the Shang.

KINGS AND EMPERORS

Ancient China was not one country, but a number of kingdoms. Sometimes one ruling family was powerful enough to control all of China. At other times, rival kingdoms fought for supremacy.

Chinese history is divided into periods, named after the ruling family or dynasty. The first dynasty we know much about was that of the Shang kings, who ruled from the 1700s B.C. After them, a succession of dynasties ruled until the 20th century, when China became a republic.

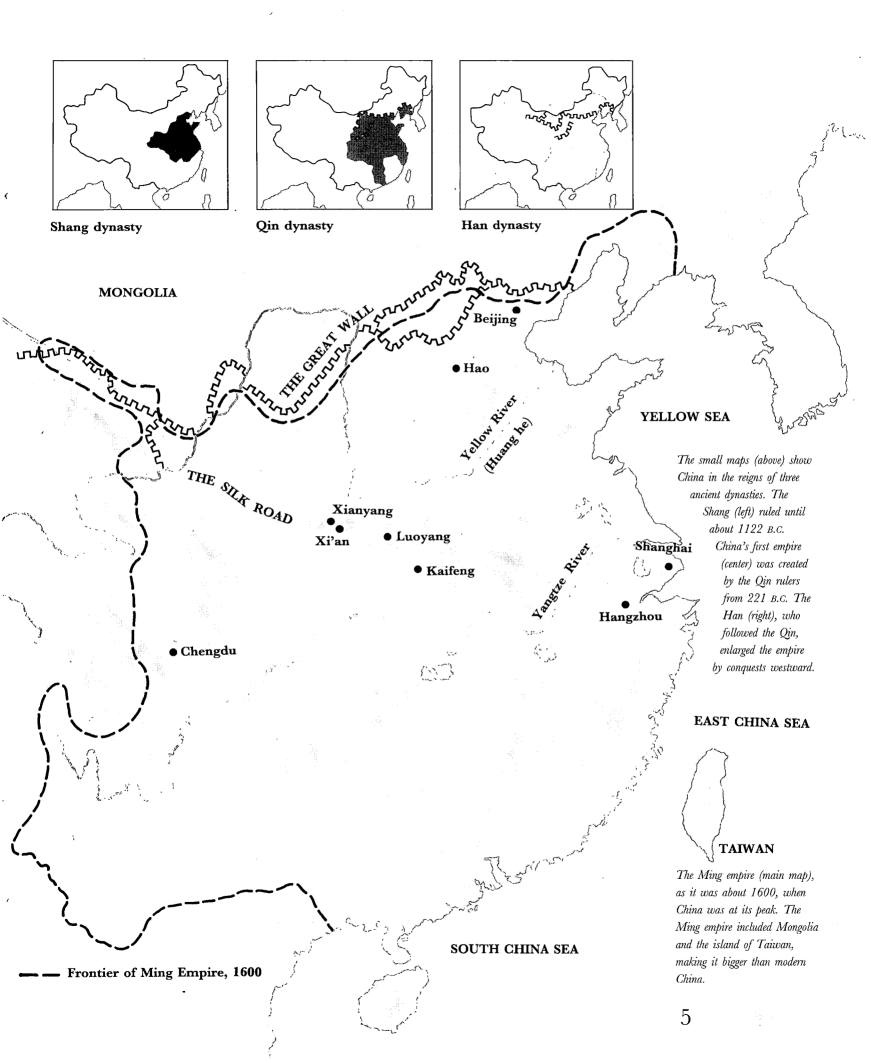

Shang dynasty

Qin dynasty

Han dynasty

MONGOLIA

THE GREAT WALL

Beijing

● Hao

Yellow River (Huang he)

YELLOW SEA

THE SILK ROAD

Xianyang

Xi'an

● Luoyang

● Kaifeng

Yangtze River

Shanghai

Hangzhou

The small maps (above) show China in the reigns of three ancient dynasties. The Shang (left) ruled until about 1122 B.C. China's first empire (center) was created by the Qin rulers from 221 B.C. The Han (right), who followed the Qin, enlarged the empire by conquests westward.

● Chengdu

EAST CHINA SEA

TAIWAN

SOUTH CHINA SEA

The Ming empire (main map), as it was about 1600, when China was at its peak. The Ming empire included Mongolia and the island of Taiwan, making it bigger than modern China.

- - - Frontier of Ming Empire, 1600

5

Shang rulers were fierce priest-kings who worshipped their ancestors, and sought their advice on important matters of state, such as where to build new cities. The bronze tools, weapons, and ornamental objects made during this time are considered some of the finest in the world.

> I have consulted the tortoise shell and obtained the reply: "This is no place to live."
>
> *—————— King Pan Geng ——————*

The Shang lived in north China. They built China's first fortified cities. These began as villages, with walls to defend people from attack by enemies. The king lived in a large hall, made from timber posts and mud-plastered walls with overhanging roofs. The homes of common people were smaller, but made in a similar style from earth and sticks. Such buildings were easy to repair or rebuild if an earthquake struck. Human bones have been found beneath Shang palaces. This suggests that human sacrifices were made when a new royal house was built.

ORACLE BONES

The Shang moved their capital to a new city at least six times. Before each move, the king asked the advice of his ancestors. Shamans, or court magicians, studied animal bones and tortoise shells to provide answers to questions concerning the future. The Shang relied on their oracles for advice on

This is a Shang fortified village. The settlement has a wall, and a gatehouse to defend the entrance. There is a communal well for drinking water. Most people live in small houses with thatched roofs, but the local lord has an impressive home.

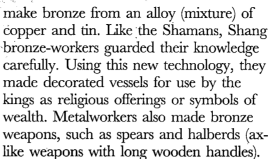

Bronze casters at work. In the background is a kiln for firing the clay molds. For large, decorated vessels, the mold was often made in several pieces. The molten bronze was poured in, and when it had cooled and hardened, the mold was broken open.

city building, warfare, planting crops, and even when was a favorable time to hunt. In 1936, scientists discovered 17,000 oracle bones in a single pit.

To divine meaning from an oracle bone, the shaman pressed a hot needle or point against the bone or shell. The heat made it crack. The pattern of the crack was believed to be a coded message, which the shaman then deciphered. He wrote down the answers to questions by scratching characters into the bone. This was the earliest known Chinese writing. At first, only the shamans could read the "magic writing," which had many characters or signs like those used to write modern Chinese. From the writings on the bones, experts have been able to read the names of Shang kings.

BRONZE CASTING
The Shang Chinese were one of the first people in the world to discover how to make bronze from an alloy (mixture) of copper and tin. Like the Shamans, Shang bronze-workers guarded their knowledge carefully. Using this new technology, they made decorated vessels for use by the kings as religious offerings or symbols of wealth. Metalworkers also made bronze weapons, such as spears and halberds (ax-like weapons with long wooden handles).

Bronze-making workshops were located close to the king's palace so the king could control the output of his skilled workers. Potters, stone masons, and jade carvers worked in similar royal workshops. Craftworkers formed a small social class. They ranked above the mass of peasant-farmers but beneath the warrior-nobles, who were the king's courtiers and generals.

COOKING POTS
Most people in China cooked food in a pot called a ding. The pot was divided inside, so that several foods could be cooked at the same time. This type of pot was first made in China during the Stone Age, from three clay pots stuck together. Shang craftworkers improved the art of pot-making. The best pots were finely decorated, but ordinary people used plain pottery.

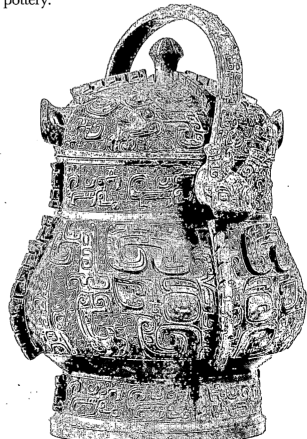

A bronze wine bucket, made during the Shang period. Its fine decoration suggests that it was probably used for important ritual ceremonies. The Shang Chinese led the world in bronze-working.

7

The see-through scene shows how people and animals were buried with the king in the pit. The complete views show how dead people and animals were placed in the pit, and what it looked like afterward, when the tomb site became a sacred spot. The detailed views show the king's burial chamber before and after workers began covering it.

A Shang king was buried with his treasures and chariots. Strewn around his tomb were the bodies of animals, human captives, and servants.

TOMBS OF ANYANG

Royal tombs discovered at Anyang revealed the splendors—and horrors—of Shang China. The burial ground of the Shang kings includes 11 royal graves and more than a thousand other tombs.

Each royal grave was a large pit, shaped like a long cross and dug facing north-south. People and animals were led down ramps into the pit and sacrificed so that they might accompany the king into the afterlife. The bodies of these captive soldiers, servants, grooms, chariot-drivers, women, horses, oxen, pigs, and deer were placed throughout the pit. Around the king's body were the goods that he would need in the next world. Placed closest to him were treasures such as

This bronze helmet is one of the many treasures found at the Shang burial ground of Anyang.

bronze cauldrons and weapons, carved jade ornaments, bone carvings, pottery, and stone sculptures. Excavators found the skeleton of a dog beneath one burial, which may have been a favorite pet or hunting companion.

HUMAN SACRIFICES

Human sacrifices were an important part of the funeral ritual. Many victims were prisoners of war. They were sometimes beheaded, and their heads laid out in a separate part of the grave as proof of the dead king's might in battle.

FILLING THE PIT

When the king's body had been laid inside, the burial chamber was roofed over. The ramps leading down to it were heaped with bronze weapons, containers of food, and ritual vessels. The bodies of more servants and captives were arranged in the pit. Then earth was thrown in, layer by layer. Each layer was pounded tightly by slaves until a solid mound of soil covered the tomb.

The funeral ceremony was led by the next king. He was usually the dead king's younger brother, not his son.

Detail:
1 Tomb containing king's body
2 Slaves laying planks to cover the burial pit
3 Sacrificed soldiers
4 Soldier guarding the pit
5 Slaves covering the pit with soil
6 More sacrificed soldiers being taken into position

Overview:
1 Central shrine
2 Raised platform
3 Priests in attendance
4 Ramp to raised platform
5 Small temples
6 Priests and holy men

Top, a ritual ax, used to kill sacrificial victims. Beneath, an oracle bone. Many inscribed animal bones, dug up in recent times by farmers, were sold as "dragon bones" for use as medicine. Experts realized that they were oracle bones, once used to foretell events.

Most of the people of China were peasant farmers. They lived by growing crops on small plots of land. Farmers were often at the mercy of the weather: droughts or floods could plunge thousands into starvation.

CROPS AND ANIMALS

The first farmers of north China's river valleys grew millet and wheat. Those in the warmer, wetter south grew rice. Farmers may have kept pigs and chickens, but there was not enough good pasture for dairy cows, so people did not have much milk or butter. They did keep oxen and water buffalo to pull carts and plows.

A Chinese peasant plowing with an ox. Horses were too valuable as war animals to be used by farmers. Instead, farmers used oxen and buffalo for heavy work.

The village was the heart of Chinese life. Much of the land was either too mountainous or too dry for crop-growing, so farmers made the most of the good land by terracing hillsides or digging irrigation ditches. In this village, peasants tend rice seedlings in a flooded field. Others work in the neat vegetable gardens.

FARMING COMMUNITIES

Several families made up farming villages. Villagers worked together for the good of the community. In the dry farmland of north and central China, villagers dug ditches and canals to water the fields. These farmers were China's first engineers.

In southern rice-growing areas, a network of ditches fed water to fields where rice seedlings were planted. Ditches also supplied water to keep fish ponds full.

Because there were few farm animals to provide manure for fertilizer, "nightsoil" (human excrement) was used instead. It was collected daily from villages and taken in carts and wheelbarrows to the fields.

COMMUNAL GRAVES

Most farming villages had a simple communal burial ground, where the graves of ancestors were set out in neat rows. The Chinese honored their ancestors with many rituals and ceremonies.

FARM TOOLS

Even after the Chinese became skilled at making bronze and iron weapons, many farmers continued to use simple wooden or stone tools. Peasants dug with wooden sticks and weeded with stone-tipped hoes, as their ancestors had done for centuries. They harvested grain with stone knives and scythes.

NEW RULERS

The Shang controlled the fertile valleys around the Yellow River. This rich farmland was very important to the empire. Peasant farmers provided the Shang with a constant food supply necessary to support their large armies. During the Shang dynasty, these armies advanced east toward the sea, and south to the Chang Jiang, or Yangtze—China's other great river. People in the conquering army's path were either driven away or quietly absorbed into the Shang culture.

The Shang kings ruled until about 1122 B.C., when warrior-kings known as the Zhou swept down from the western mountains and conquered them. The Zhou became China's new rulers.

The lives of peasant farmers consisted of many long, back-breaking hours tending to their crops. Most had little time in their day-to-day activities to concern themselves with the comings and going of kings. Only in times of great distress, such as during long droughts that brought starvation, would the peasants rise up against the wealthy landowners.

The painting above dates from the 13th or 14th century and shows Chinese farmers irrigating rice fields. One is using a pole and bucket device to lift water; the others are working a treadmill. Rice was first grown in southern China, probably before 3000 B.C. The picture below shows a man harvesting with a scythe.

11

China became a feudal society under the Zhou conquerors. The king gave land to nobles in return for their loyalty and service. The nobles were lords of their own territories, with absolute power over their subjects, most of whom were peasants.

Scholars were the only people who could read and write. Some taught the sons of nobles. Others traveled from town to town, or worked as government officials.

FEUDAL CHINA

Each noble built castles and walled towns to defend his land against attack. Peasant farmers worked the noble's land. They also served as soldiers in the noble's armies. In exchange for their fidelity, the lord protected the peasants in times of attack. But the peasants were essentially slaves to the lord in everything but name.

A noble's utmost goal was to win and keep the favor of the king. He did this by demonstrating his allegiance to the royal family whenever possible, most often by fighting the king's enemies with his armies of peasant-soldiers.

The Chinese aristocracy had various ranks, from "dukes" at the top to "barons" at the bottom. Below these

A miller uses a grindstone to grind rice. Milling removes the hard covering, or hull, which is too tough to eat.

noblemen were smaller landowners and scholars. Next came the peasant farmers and craftworkers. Merchants were the lowest-ranking class in China, until the Song Empire (from A.D. 960.)

ROYAL POWER WEAKENS

In time the Zhou kings lost the loyalty of the nobles. In 771 B.C., the Zhou capital of Hao was attacked by nomad tribes from Mongolia. The Zhou king fled, and in the confusion that followed, the strongest nobles set up their own states.

THE WARRING STATES

For the next five hundred years, warring states struggled for power in China. But despite the fighting, China prospered. There were more people, more food was grown, and new tools made of iron replaced many of the softer bronze ones.

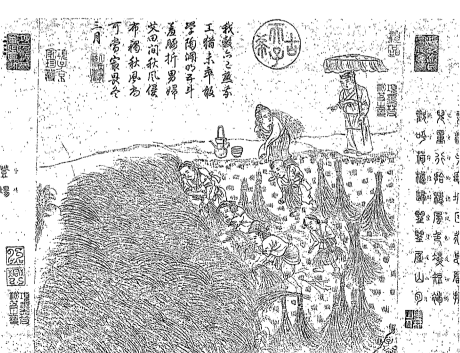

The lord's steward comes to inspect the rice harvest. This painting dates from when the Mongols ruled China, but farm methods had changed little in hundreds of years.

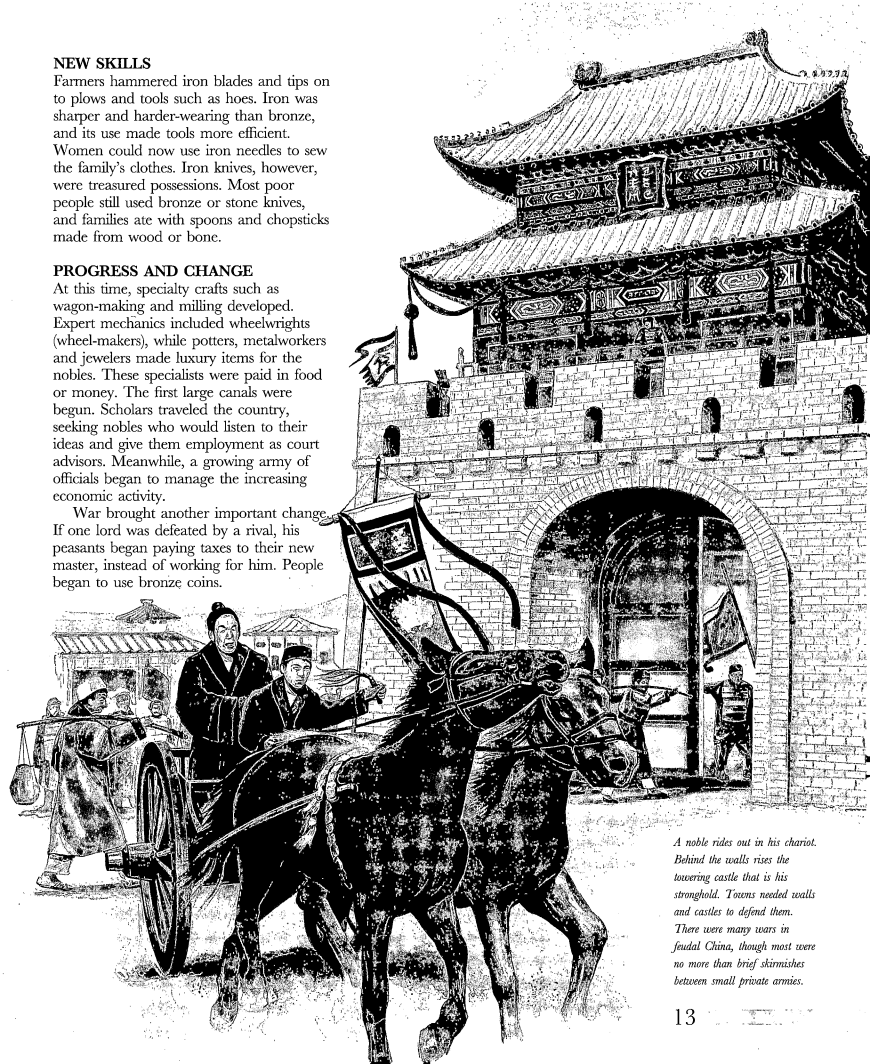

NEW SKILLS

Farmers hammered iron blades and tips on to plows and tools such as hoes. Iron was sharper and harder-wearing than bronze, and its use made tools more efficient. Women could now use iron needles to sew the family's clothes. Iron knives, however, were treasured possessions. Most poor people still used bronze or stone knives, and families ate with spoons and chopsticks made from wood or bone.

PROGRESS AND CHANGE

At this time, specialty crafts such as wagon-making and milling developed. Expert mechanics included wheelwrights (wheel-makers), while potters, metalworkers and jewelers made luxury items for the nobles. These specialists were paid in food or money. The first large canals were begun. Scholars traveled the country, seeking nobles who would listen to their ideas and give them employment as court advisors. Meanwhile, a growing army of officials began to manage the increasing economic activity.

War brought another important change. If one lord was defeated by a rival, his peasants began paying taxes to their new master, instead of working for him. People began to use bronze coins.

A noble rides out in his chariot. Behind the walls rises the towering castle that is his stronghold. Towns needed walls and castles to defend them. There were many wars in feudal China, though most were no more than brief skirmishes between small private armies.

13

> A man who returns from battle
> with five heads is made the master
> of five families.
>
> — *Xunzi*

War in ancient China began with personal duels between rival nobles that followed strict rules of chivalry. But by the **300s** B.C., the Chinese had new and deadlier weapons, and their large, well-equipped armies engaged in savage warfare. The philosopher Xunzi was shocked by the new militarism.

Peasant soldiers did not wear armor, and carried wooden shields. In battle, such troops were no match for better-armed infantry and horsemen with swords and bows.

Part of the terracotta model army from Emperor Shi Huang-di's tomb of about 210 B.C.

THE WARRING STATES

Chinese historians divided the long years of war into two periods: the Spring and Autumn Period (770–485 B.C.) and the Warring States Period (485–221 B.C.). In the first period, there were many small states, each ruled by a prince. In the second, the strongest states gradually defeated their weaker rivals until only seven states remained. Of these, the most powerful were Qin and Chu.

NEW METHODS OF WAR

These two states defeated their enemies with armies larger than any seen in China before. They sent as many as 100,000 men into battle. Towns were besieged for months. The Qin were particularly ruthless. There was no place for the old noble codes of honor and chivalry. After one victory, Qin generals executed 400,000 prisoners. ·

Some traditions remained. A Chinese general still consulted oracles and prayed to his ancestors for aid before a battle.

NOMAD ATTACKS

While the states fought one another, China also faced attacks from outside. From the north and west came raids by the nomads. These were cavalry soldiers, lightly armored but riding fast horses. To counter their raids, the Chinese built a number of frontier walls. These walls would later be merged into the famous Great Wall.

CROSSBOWS AND BOWS

During the fourth century B.C., the Chinese developed a new and formidable long-range weapon, the crossbow. This was more powerful than the bow used by chariot warriors. It also had a skillfully made trigger mechanism. Crossbows were ideal for shooting from behind a wall against an onrushing enemy. The weapon could fire arrows as far as 650 feet to rip through a wooden shield. It was deadly accurate. Not even a mounted knight stood much chance against a well-trained crossbowman.

The composite bow used by archers and charioteers was also very effective. It was made of strips of wood or bone lashed together, and fired arrows tipped with bone, bronze, or iron heads.

ARMOR

Much of what we know about Chinese soldiers comes from studies of the terracotta warriors found in the tomb of the first Qin emperor. These life-size figures reveal small details. For example, soldiers wore linen scarves to prevent their armor from rubbing their necks. Armor was made of plates of metal or leather, fastened together.

OTHER WEAPONS

The first Chinese swords were short, and had a handgrip bound with cord. But as metal-working improved, swords over three feet long were made. Before the first century A.D., most of these weapons were made of bronze, but later there were swords of iron and even steel. The Chinese also made chromium-plated, nonrusting swords, found nowhere else in the ancient world. One such sword dug up by archaeologists was still sharp enough to cut a hair, after spending 2,000 years in the ground.

The halberd, or ko, was used in hand-to-hand combat before swords became more common. The halberd was a thick wooden shaft about six feet long, tipped with an ax-like blade.

Such weapons predominated until the Song dynasty (A.D. 960), during which gunpowder was invented. Then bombs and rockets brought a new sound and fury to the battlefield.

A model of a Chinese cavalryman of the Tang empire (A.D. 618–907). Horse and rider are heavily armored. The Chinese went to great lengths to obtain cavalry horses. They especially prized western horses that were bigger and faster than the sturdy ponies of China.

THE FIRST EMPEROR

The leader of the Qin, Prince Sheng, became ruler of all China in 221 B.C. He was the first emperor to control the entire country and he set out to rule it as he ruled Qin. Qin was now the strongest of all China's kingdoms. It had a firm central government, efficient irrigation systems and farming, and a powerful army. The name China came from Qin.

Work on the Great Wall. Elephants were brought in to help with the heavy labor, but most of the soil and stones were shifted by human hands.

UNIFYING CHINA

Prince Sheng was known as the "Tiger of Qin." He was ambitious and ruthless. Having defeated his rivals, he took a new name: Shi Huang-di, meaning "First Emperor," and set about unifying China. He ordered all his people to speak the same language. He standardized the system of weights and measurements, and established one coinage. There was even a standard width for carts using the new roads that the emperor had ordered built to speed up communications.

All over China, noble families were made responsible for law and order in their own region, and for seeing that the emperor's word was obeyed. Ordinary citizens had to serve as soldiers and help to build the new roads, canals, and fortifications.

THE GREAT WALL

One of the emperor's mightiest projects was the initial construction of the Great Wall, sometimes known as the "longest cemetery in the world" because so many people died while laboring to build it.

The purpose of the Wall was to protect China's northern borders from invasion. Construction was planned to link up shorter lengths of the old defensive walls that had been built over the previous few hundred years.

The project was run like an army. Supply camps were set up to ferry food and materials to the mountains and deserts of the northern frontier. Soldiers were posted to the vast building site to fight off bandits and to stop workers from running away. Thousands of peasants were marched from their fields to work on the Wall. Many of them never returned home. One consequence of this was that crops were neglected and many people went hungry.

While subsequent emperors rebuilt and extended the Wall, the project was so vast that the majority of the construction did not even take place until centuries later, during the Ming dynasty.

THE EMPEROR'S TOMB

The emperor's own tomb was another huge project, on which 700,000 people toiled for almost 40 years. Craftsmen worked in factories to make the terracotta army of soldiers and horses left to guard the emperor in death.

Shi Huang-di made his capital at Xianyang and kept his nobles at court, where he could keep an eye on them.

A BREAK WITH THE PAST

The First Emperor was determined to destroy all ideas from the past and ordered books of "literature, history, and discussion" to be burned. Only "useful" books, such as texts on medicine and agriculture, were spared. Scholars who continued to support the old traditions were banished or executed.

Shi Huang-di was feared by his people, but he was never loved. When he died at the age of 49, his family did not reign long after him. Liu Bang, a soldier of humble birth, fought his way to power and became emperor in 202 B.C. He took the name Han Gaozu. During the Han dynasty, China recovered from the upheavals of the First Emperor's rule.

These are Chinese coins. Early coins had holes drilled in them so that they could be hung on strings. Before round or oval shaped coins came into use, the Chinese used coins shaped like spades and knives.

The Chinese did not follow one religion. They believed the emperor was a god, and also worshipped their ancestors and various spirits of the home and countryside. Most people were ready to mix ancient beliefs with new ideas such as Buddhism, from India. Chinese philosophers such as Confucius taught the right way to live and govern.

An 18th-century picture of Confucius with his followers. He believed in order and respect for tradition. He taught that a ruler must follow the right principles, established in ancient times. By following these principles, humans could progress.

This painting on a wood panel comes from Chinese Turkestan, and was made in the sixth to seventh centuries. It shows Roustein, God of Silk.

CONFUCIUS
Confucius is the westernized name for the teacher Kong Qiu, who earned the title Kongfusi—"Great Master Kong."
He failed to become an important court advisor, but his teachings were collected by his followers and became principles for good government and personal behavior. His sayings—such as "If we are not to live with our fellow men, with whom can we live?"—were familiar to all Chinese. In 124 B.C. the Imperial University was set up to teach Confucianism to future government officials.

TAOISM
Confucius was concerned mostly with laws made by people, and whether people were naturally good or naturally evil. In contrast, the followers of Lao-tzu believed people were guided by universal laws, not human ones. This was the basis of Taoism.

Knowledge studies others.
Wisdom is self-known.

——————— *Lao-tzu* ———————

During the fighting of the Warring States Period, thinkers and teachers traveled around China seeking employment from nobles. Among the most famous teachers were Confucius (551–479 B.C.) and his disciples Mencius (371–289 B.C.) and Xunzi (315–236 B.C.); and Lao-tzu (c.500 B.C.). These great philosophers were concerned more with good government and personal behavior than with spiritual gods or "heaven and hell."

Tao means "the Way" and the Taoists tried to lead a simple life of meditation, close to nature. Taoism was mystical and influenced by ancient Chinese folk religion. Its followers used magic as well as prayer and diet to seek eternal youth.

This 12th-century painting illustrates the virtues of a son's obedience. Fathers expected their sons to honor them as ancestors, and so support them in the next life.

YIN AND YANG

The Chinese believed that there was a balance in nature. This came from the idea that there were two forces in everything: yin and yang. Yang was strong, active, bright, and male. Yin was weak, passive, dark, and female. The two were opposites, but neither could exist without the other. The concept of Yin and Yang was represented by a circle with interlinking black and white halves.

BUDDHISM

Buddhism came to China from India in the first century A.D., when the emperor sent for copies of Buddhist writings. Scholars read these with interest. Buddhist teachings also came from Southeast Asia, through trading contacts.

Buddhism and Taoism had much in common: both believed in everlasting life through self-discipline and meditation. Chinese emperors employed Buddhist counselors for their political advice and their supposed magical skills.

19

T he Chinese believed they were a favored people, superior to all other cultures. The basis of Chinese life was a belief in harmony and balance. It affected the food people chose to eat, the times at which they did things, and even the way they planned their buildings.

A wedding procession. Brides presented a gift, or dowry, to their husband and his family. A couple with the same surname were forbidden to marry, in case they shared the same ancestor. A man had one lawful wife, but some nobles (and the emperor) also had concubines or secondary wives. These ranked below the legal wife.

LIVING IN HARMONY

The Chinese belief in living in harmony with nature affected their everyday life in many ways. It was linked to a belief that every place had its own natural spirits. Some spirits dwelt in the mountains, rivers, rain, and wind. Others were found in and around the house—in the stove, in the well, in the vegetable garden. People tried to keep on good terms with the spirits and sometimes honored them with gifts and included them in feasts and rituals.

The Chinese believed the souls of the dead returned, just as the caterpillar of the silk moth changed its form during the insect's life cycle. Many people readily accepted the Buddhist idea of rebirth.

FAMILY LIFE

The family held Chinese society together. An old written character meaning "what is good" was made from a picture showing a woman with children. Families in China usually included many generations living together—often under the same roof. Children were taught to respect and obey their elders.

This Chinese painting from the 12th century shows followers of Buddha distributing gifts to the poor.

MEN AND WOMEN

Men were seen as superior to women. Parents believed they would become gods after they died if they had a son. They rejoiced if a son was born, but might kill a newborn female. Only sons could go to school, and only a son could inherit property. Upper-class women followed the painful custom of footbinding. Cloth strips were wrapped around a girl's feet to bend her toes all the way under to the arches, making the foot appear tiny. Over time, binding deformed the feet, and made it very difficult for a woman to walk. Small feet were considered delicate and feminine, and were thought to make a woman more eligible for marriage.

FESTIVALS

The Chinese calendar was based on the moon, and divided years into groups of 12, each named after an animal. The most important festival each year was the Chinese New Year, a spring festival, during which offerings were made to the spirits: the god of the household stove was offered sweets so he would not tell of any mischief he might have seen in the old year.

Most marriages were arranged. In this 19th-century painting, families celebrate a wedding. After the wedding, the bride went to live with her husband's family. There was a ceremony to worship her husband's ancestors and his family's household gods. Then she humbly offered tea to her new family.

DEATH AND FUNERALS

At a Chinese funeral, people wore white, the color of mourning. Children showed respect for dead parents by fasting and wearing thick clothing.

During the funeral, wooden and clay models of objects such as houses and boats were placed in tombs. The dead were given food and drink to enjoy in the next world. Nobles were buried with silk robes, painted bowls and boxes, wooden models of their servants, cosmetics, and false hair to make them look young. People visited family graves in spring and autumn with offerings of food.

The Chinese believed it was important to preserve the body. A tomb from 113 B.C. contained the remains of a prince and his wife wearing suits of jade. Each suit was made from 2,000 pieces of jade, sewn together with gold and silk-covered iron wire. Jade was believed to have magical powers to preserve the body, but only dust remained inside these suits.

For the Chinese, art could be enjoyed in private or as part of a public ritual. They loved poetry, pictures, folktales, music, and dance. Everyday objects of clay, metal, and jade were shaped with great care. The finest pieces, from Shang bronzes to Ming vases, were crafted with skills unsurpassed anywhere in the world.

PAINTING

From the 400s B.C., Chinese painters made exquisite pictures on silk. Artists later painted on paper, a Chinese invention. Landscapes were popular from the tenth century A.D. Calm scenes of mountains, rivers, and waterfalls showed the harmony between nature and people. Such paintings expressed the same ideas as those of philosophers and poets. Artists also painted animals, including fish, birds, and insects, as well as portraits of people.

Chinese artists were also skilled in calligraphy—delicate handwriting, using a fine-tipped brush and ink. This art was considered as important as painting.

Part of the Diamond Sutra, or scroll, one of the oldest printed books known. It was made in China in A.D. 868. Seven sheets were pasted together to form a scroll, and each sheet was printed from a carved woodblock. The text contains Buddhist teachings.

The First Emperor was buried with an army of more than 7,000 terracotta model soldiers and horses. Teams of workers assembled the clay models from ready-made sections.

POTTERY AND SILKS

Chinese potters made clay pots on wheels as long ago as 2000 B.C. Later, in the Tang dynasty, the Chinese made the world's first porcelain. This fine, painted pottery became known in the West as "china." Chinese pottery and silks were greatly valued by foreigners. After European sailors began visiting China in the 16th century A.D., trade in such goods increased. Chinese styles for gardens, pottery, and furnishings became fashionable in Europe and were copied by Western designers. In the Song dynasty, workers perfected silk-weaving on looms, copying paintings into silk tapestry.

SCULPTURE AND JEWELRY

During the Han dynasty, large stone statues were set up outside tombs. When Buddhism reached China, enormous rock statues of Buddha were made. Some of these figures were more than 30 feet high, yet they were as detailed as if the artist had painted them with a fine brush. In the Song dynasty, sculptors carved handsome wooden figures, while the tombs of Ming emperors were guarded by massive stone beasts.

With equal skill, artists worked on intricate jade carvings and objects made in gold and silver. Often an artist copied older styles, so that a piece made in the 12th century looked the same as one made more than a thousand years before.

LITERATURE AND DRAMA

The oldest forms of Chinese literature were poems and songs. Some were recited at weddings and rituals. The main books of Confucianism—the Five Classics—were regarded as ideal writing.

Han writers excelled in recording history. The greatest Chinese poets lived during the Tang dynasty (A.D. 618–907). They included Wang Wei, Li Po, and Tu Fu. Poets wrote about love, the pleasures of drink, and the senselessness of war. The Chinese were the first to print books, from the ninth century A.D.

Drama developed during the 13th century A.D. A Chinese drama combined singing and dancing, somewhat like an opera. Stories were often based on ancient

Artists painted people at work. This silk painting of the 15th or 16th century shows a man fishing with cormorants. Chinese fishermen still use these diving birds to catch fish.

folk tales. People also read fiction. The most famous novel is *The Journey to the West* (or *Monkey*) by Wu Cheng-en.

MUSIC

Chinese music uses a five-tone scale instead of the eight-tone scale of Western music. Music was played at court and in city streets. Drums, gongs, and pipes were common instruments.

Pottery models of two princesses, from the Tang period (7th–10th centuries). They are dressed in the height of fashion, with elaborate hairstyles, enormous sleeves and turned-up shoes in the form of a lotus.

Part of the silk embroidery of the Blue Dragon Robe, the official costume of the imperial family and its officials. It was made in the 19th century. The bats are good-luck symbols. Various Chinese characters were woven into the design, including the signs for joy and fortune.

23

A NOBLEMAN'S HOUSE

Home was important to the Chinese nobleman. His house showed his wealth and rank in society. This picture is reconstructed from clay models of houses found in Han tombs. The models were intended to make the dead person "at home" when he or she entered the next world.

Most Chinese houses were built of wood, with a timber frame to hold up the roof. The outer walls were made of brick or of a lighter material. This might be bamboo wattle plastered over with clay or pounded earth. Inner walls were plastered and sometimes painted.

The Chinese preferred wood to stone for building. They thought stone was somehow "unnatural." Wood was also less likely to injure the occupants if the building collapsed in an earthquake. There are few really old buildings in China. Emperors built new palaces to replace old ones, and most old houses were knocked down to make way for new buildings.

This building had overhanging eaves, which are common in China. They let water run off clear of the walls, and gave welcome shade in the summer. The ends of the roof supports were often upturned and decorated.

A wealthy noble could afford tiles on his roof. Ordinary people made do with straw thatch.

The house of a nobleman was larger than the single-story home of a farmer. It was an elegant pavilion, built with several floors that were linked by stairs. Around the house there was a wall enclosing a courtyard. Visitors entered a town house through a gate from the street. The entrance to a country villa was from surrounding fields. Inside the walls there was usually a garden with shrubs, and often a fish pond.

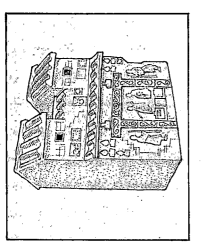

Pottery models of houses, like this one, were placed in tombs, as symbols of the dead person's status and for use in the afterlife. The see-through scene shows how a house of the Han period was built, and what the inside was like.

1 Timber framework of house
2 Outer walls of brick or dried clay
3 Overhanging roof eaves
4 Typical roof decoration
5 Tiled roof—a sign of wealth
6 Topmost roof—a watchtower and a place for quiet study
7 Upper rooms for meeting guests
8 Men playing a board game
9 Lady with a maidservant
10 Food being served
11 Tiled entrance hall

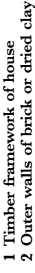

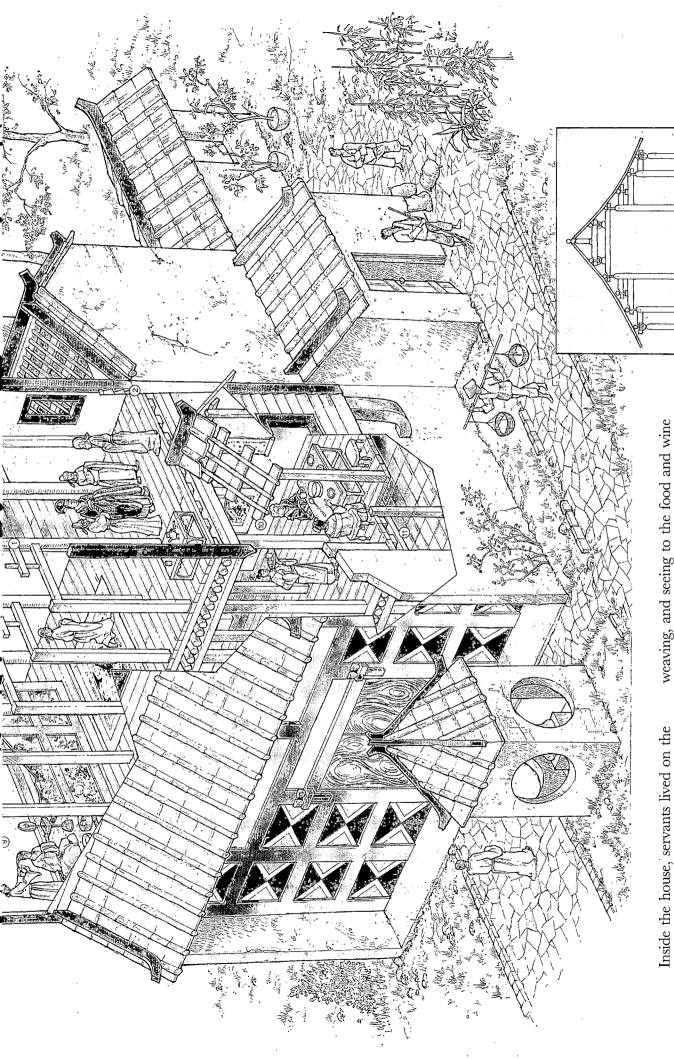

Inside the house, servants lived on the ground floor, where the kitchen was placed. (Poor people often cooked outside their homes, in the open air.) The noble used the rooms above for meeting friends, dining, and attending to his business affairs. Women and children might use the upper rooms, from where they could look down into the street. The women performed domestic tasks such as sewing,

weaving, and seeing to the food and wine served to guests. When they went out, they rode in a horse-drawn carriage or were carried in litters by servants.

The topmost tower room gave the house a military look. The Han nobles were famous soldiers, and the design of the house is a reminder of times when the noble's house would have been a stronghold as well as a home.

A typical Chinese house was made of timber or bamboo poles, which supported the sloping roof. The side walls did not carry weight. They were made from light materials, easy to replace, and were often plastered over.

Chinese cities were larger than any others in the world. In medieval Europe, cities grew so powerful that their leaders sometimes challenged the power of kings. In China, the city was a symbol of the emperor's power. Peasants in the fields might grumble, but few of China's city dwellers ever rose in revolt.

NEW RULER, NEW CITY

When a new dynasty came to power, its ruler usually ordered the building of a new capital city. For example, Chang'an in northern China was chosen by the first Han emperor to replace the old imperial capital of Xianyang.

Like all Chinese cities, Chang'an was well protected by walls more than 12 miles long. These were 60 feet high in places and up to 50 feet thick. Inside, people felt safe from attack.

IMPERIAL CITY

The Emperor and his court lived in the center and south of the city. The imperial craftworkers and servants lived in the northwest. Everyone else lived in the northeast, while merchants lived outside the city walls altogether.

Chang'an was China's imperial capital more than once. It was destroyed in A.D. 25, but became the capital again in the sixth century A.D. Much rebuilding was needed. A main road over 475 feet wide was laid through the city. This created two sections, each with its own market and its own police. The city was further split into blocks by tree-lined avenues. There were public parks and open spaces.

Chang'an was the biggest city in the world, bigger than even Rome. As many as a million people lived there, and governing the city was complicated. For example, there were 400 or so market traders to be checked by city officials, who

Street traders were found in all China's cities. This old print by a European artist shows customers eating at a street-side restaurant in Macao.

A detail from an ink drawing on silk called "Going up the River at the Spring Festival." Dating from the Song period (about 1100), it shows a lively view of a city, probably Kaifeng. Camels, horses, and a litter carried by servants pass by. Shoppers and traders do business at stalls below the tall buildings.

A busy scene in Chang'an, more than a thousand years ago. Travelers from distant regions, farmers, and merchants arrived every day. Graceful bridges spanned canals. Towers and fine houses lined the streets. By day and night, restaurants and teahouses were crowded as people enjoyed the many entertainments the city had to offer.

made sure that fair weights of food were sold. Streets became known for their trades (such as fish, poultry, medicines, pots, and so on). Traders formed guilds or unions to look after their interests.

CITY LIFE

Other cities grew to rival Chang'an in size. They included Kaifeng, the northern Song capital (960–1126), and Hangzhou (capital from 1128 to 1276), which Marco Polo visited. These cities were not planned as well as Chang'an. They were overcrowded, with fewer open spaces. The many wooden buildings packed together led to frequent fires. Beggars, thieves, and pickpockets were numerous. But cities attracted rich people and their luxuries. Even Marco Polo, who came from the splendors of Venice, was impressed by what he saw in Hangzhou.

TOWN AND COUNTRY

Most Chinese people lived in country villages. Peasants going to town to sell their goods at market looked in awe at the town houses, with their tiled roofs, and the busy teahouses. They marveled at the music, puppet shows, and magicians.

Poor people spent most of their time growing and preparing food, or doing heavy work such as digging and load-carrying. They had little spare time and no money to spend on luxuries such as fine clothes. The well-to-do lived comfortably, enjoying the pleasures of their houses and gardens. Rich and poor had different pastimes.

FOOD

The Chinese believed that their diet should be linked to how they felt. A cook might change the menu, or the way food was prepared depending on the family's health, or even if the weather changed.

For poor people, daily meals were simple. Their main foods were rice, millet, vegetables, and beans. If they ate meat, it may have been a chicken or wild bird. Fish was a tasty extra, caught from ponds, rivers, or canals.

A VARIED MENU

Wealthy families had a wider choice of foods, with meats of various kinds (pork, lamb, venison, duck, goose, pigeon). Other animals to appear on the table might include snakes, dogs, snails, sparrows, or bear paws, which were a delicacy. Cooks prepared meals using spices such as ginger and cinnamon, and used salt, sugar, honey, and soy sauce to add flavor. Favorite dishes included honey rolls, steamed bread (steaming was a common cooking method), and noodles. Vegetables and fruit were always on the table. There were regional variations in cooking that utilized local produce and meats.

People usually drank tea, and seldom drank water without boiling it. Another popular drink was rice wine.

Townspeople bought drinks and snacks from street stalls. They could enjoy tea, cakes, bread, or a hot breakfast of sausages.

Detail from a 12th-century painting, showing scholars enjoying a meal in a garden. Tea is being prepared by servants.

KEEPING WARM OR COOL

In winter, people wore thick padded clothing. Warm clothing was especially needed in north China, where winters can be very cold. In their homes people burned charcoal or coal on their fires. Hot air from the cooking stove was piped through hollow bricks to warm seats and beds. In the heat of summer, houses could be very stuffy. Then people took out the waxed paper sheets that covered the windows to let in more fresh air. Wealthy ladies fanned themselves with elegantly painted paper fans. In summer, people often ate outdoors.

KEEPING CLEAN

The Chinese enjoyed baths, and washed with soap made from herbs. Most townspeople paid a small fee to use one of the public baths. The houses of the rich had private bathrooms, but the poor had to make do with communal drains and latrines. Yet, foreign travelers found Chinese cities impressively clean. Hot water for washing was sold in the street, and all waste was collected by night and carted away outside the walls. The Chinese also used toilet paper, a habit that surprised foreign visitors.

GAMES AND PETS

When the day's work was over, poor people enjoyed storytelling and gambling. The Chinese played card games and chess, a game they learned from India. In the Chinese game of mah-jongg, players use small tiles with pictures or symbols on them, instead of cards.

Nobles hunted and raced horses. Noble-women grew and arranged flowers, or tended miniature trees (bonsai). Lapdogs such as the Pekingese were popular pets with ladies. A poor family might keep a songbird or a cricket in a cage.

In China, as in other countries, a person's clothes identified their social status. The emperor and nobles (left) wore elegant silk and cotton robes, and furs in winter. Merchants dressed for travel, while the scholar's gown (center) distinguished him as a person of dignity. Peasants (right) wore coarse undyed cloth that was warm in winter.

TRADE AND TRAVEL

For a time in the 1400s, China was a great sea power, as well as Asia's mightiest land empire. Chinese ships sailed as far as east Africa. But it was the land route known as the Silk Road that was China's main trade link with the Western world. The traveling merchants carried news and ideas, as well as goods.

A mariner's compass. Chinese sailors were the first to use the magnetic compass for navigation.

CHINA AND THE WORLD

China's main concern was to keep out its northern enemies. Its emperors felt secure behind the Great Wall and cared little for other empires beyond it. In 138 B.C. the emperor Wu sent an expedition west as far as Afghanistan. There the Chinese were astonished to see cities and to experience the great civilizations of the Persians, Greeks, Romans, and Indians.

About A.D. 100, a Chinese army of 70,000 men traveled west to the Caspian Sea. This huge expedition came close to the Roman Empire, but the Chinese did not make direct contact with the Romans. Instead, they were ready to trade by means of traveling merchants. The most valued item of trade was silk.

Merchants discuss a deal. Along the Silk Road, goods were sold from one merchant to another. Silk eventually reached the Persians, who controlled the western end of the silk trade. Bales of silk, ivory, jade, spices, and other goods were packed onto camels for the long journey. The merchants traveled in groups or caravans for protection against bandits, winding their way across high mountains, windswept plateaus, and deserts that were hot by day and bitterly cold by night.

The animals used by traders were two-humped Bactrian camels, which are surefooted and withstand heat or cold.

30

THE SECRET OF SILK

Silk is a fiber used to make cloth. The fiber comes from the cocoon of the silkworm (the caterpillar of the silk moth). Silk cloth is very fine. It is strong, but also warm, light, and soft.

The Chinese discovered how to make silk over 3,000 years ago and they guarded the secret closely. No one in Europe knew how to make silk until the ninth century A.D.

THE SILK ROAD

Venice

Rome

Chang'an

This map shows the route of the Silk Road. The western end of the route was the ports of Venice and Rome in Italy. It then crossed the Near East and Central Asia to China. By the time Marco Polo traveled it in the 13th century, Mongol rule had made the Silk Road safer than it had been for hundreds of years. There were inns and rest stations along the way.

THE SILK ROUTE

Foreign rulers were willing to pay high prices for colored silks from China. Getting silk to the west took many months of difficult travel across Asia, but the high price paid made it worthwhile for the merchants who risked the journey.

Silk was carried along a trail that became known as the Silk Road, and was the most famous overland trade route of ancient times. Goods sent along the Silk Road changed hands many times along the way. Few merchants traveled the whole route. Among those who did was Marco Polo, who journeyed to China from Europe in the 13th century.

VOYAGES TO AFRICA

The Chinese also sent ships abroad. From 1405 to 1433, the admiral Cheng Ho led seven voyages. His fleets were huge, with as many as 300 ships and 27,000 men. He visited Southeast Asia, Sri Lanka, India, the Middle East, and Egypt, and explored the coast of East Africa. The Chinese demanded that local rulers pay tribute to the emperor. But they did not set up colonies, as European voyagers did in the 16th century.

The Chinese had little interest in goods offered by foreigners, except gold and silver. What could foreigners supply that China did not already have?

From Venice (shown in this painting), merchants sailed to the eastern Mediterranean coast where the overland route to China began. The Silk Road was over 3,700 miles long from Persia across central Asia to the Great Wall.

The small pictures show the stages in moving a boat between levels, over a slipway. First the boat moved onto the ramp (below). The windlass hauled it higher until its front was raised into the air (below right). For a moment, the boat balanced precariously between the levels. Now turn the see-through page to see how it then tipped forward (below), and slid into the water at the higher level (right).

The Chinese relied on water transport to carry goods around China. They built a network of canals, and invented slipways and locks to move canal boats up or down between levels. Huge sailing ships called junks carried cargoes around the coasts.

CANALS ACROSS CHINA

The Chinese used canals to move food and military supplies. Building canals like the Cheng Kuo (246 B.C.) gave Qin rulers an advantage in their campaigns.

Canals also helped to unify China. The New Pien Canal (A.D. 618) linked north and south, by joining sections of old canals. The first length of the Grand Canal was opened in A.D. 610. Along it, boats carried grain from the farms around the Chang Jiang (Yangtze) River to Kaifeng and Luoyang. In the 13th century, the Mongol rulers of China extended the Grand Canal northward as far as Beijing— to speed up grain supplies and make sure they controlled the Yangtze River valley. The Ming rulers built a larger canal along the same route, which is still used today.

1 Cargo being unloaded from hold of boat
2 Small boat in low water below slipway
3 Inclined plane or slipway
4 Windlass to pull up boats
5 Canal office and storehouse
6 Boat sliding off ramp into water at the higher level

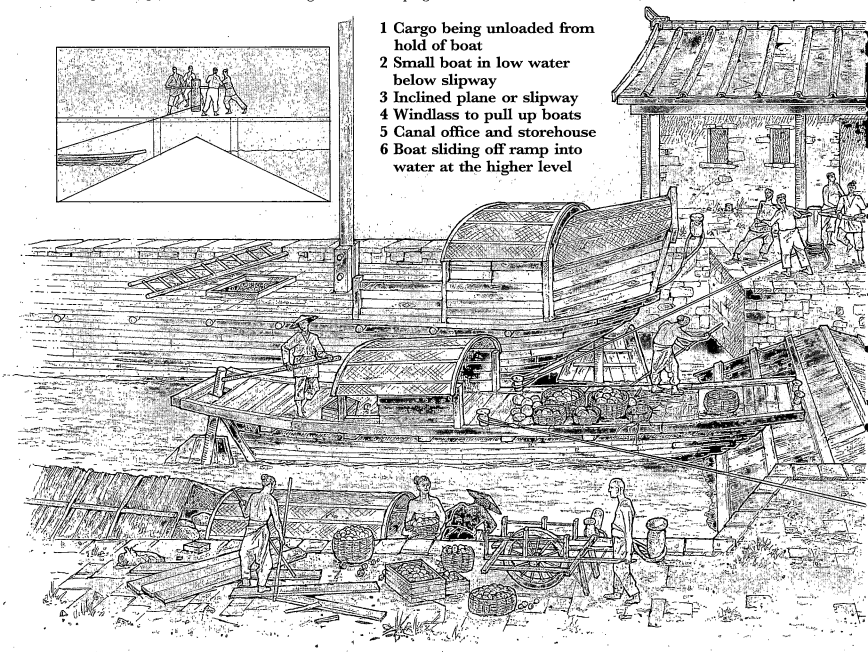

CHANGING LEVELS

Chinese engineers generally dug canals on level ground, so there were few changes in water level. About every three miles they installed flash-locks. These were sluice gates that used a simple log-stop to control the water flow. To change levels, boats were hauled up a two-sided slipway, using a windlass. This could damage the boat as it toppled over the top of the slipway. Looters sometimes stole the cargo.

Later, in the tenth century, the more advanced pound-lock was developed. Like a modern canal lock, it had gates at each end, and could be emptied or flooded as needed to lower or raise a boat between levels. Water levels could differ by three feet or more at each lock. So a series of locks allowed a canal to rise 100 feet or more above sea level.

RISE AND FALL OF CANALS

Locks made it possible to extend the canal system into new areas, and helped to prevent canals from drying out in hot summers. Barges weighing over 100 tons were in use by 1100. By the time the canal lock was copied in Europe in the late 14th century, China's canal system was being used less.

SEAGOING SHIPS

After the Mongol emperors made Beijing (Peking) their capital in the late 13th century, more and more cargoes were taken north in seagoing ships.

The Chinese built excellent sailing ships. Their biggest junks were larger than any medieval European vessel. They were stronger, and with rudders at their stern, they were easier to sail. There were numerous smaller craft, built equally strongly of timber and bamboo.

This see-through picture shows canal boats using a slipway to pass through a lock. One flat-bottomed boat is being heaved over a slipway from a lower level (left) to a higher level (right). The scene also shows how Chinese boats were built. The same basic design was used for small river boats and ocean-going junks. The boat has a strong hull with a stern rudder. The locks became busy staging posts for water trade. Boxes and bales of goods wait for shipment. Porters use wheelbarrows and yokes to carry loads, and boat owners bargain with customers over payment for the next trip.

The emperor with his officials. Civil servants and members of his family were the only people allowed direct personal contact with China's ruler.

He behaved with the utmost cruelty. . . . He ordered that all relatives, both by the father's and the mother's side, should be seized and executed.

—— *Official history of Emperor Yong Le, 1402* ——

Walled within his capital city and surrounded by officials and generals, the emperor of China was a remote figure. In the royal court, he was treated with godlike reverence. Officials of China's civil service ran the government.

FAMILY PROBLEMS

The emperor had officials and ministers to advise him and carry out his wishes. But his power was absolute. He was usually feared rather than loved, and people in his court plotted to gain his confidence.

A new emperor often feared his own family most. For a Chinese emperor, choosing a wife was a difficult problem. He could not marry a foreign princess, as China had few close links with foreign countries, and no foreigner was considered of suitable rank. So he had to choose a

wife from among the noble families of the court. Too often, his wife's relatives tried to dominate the court and even plotted against him. The emperor Wu (140–86 B.C.) took the drastic step of executing his wife's entire family!

COURT ENTERTAINMENT
Everyone was anxious to please the emperor, and he was entertained lavishly. In the 15th century the imperial kitchen staff numbered 5,000 servants and cooks. Musicians, singers, and dancers helped pass the time between meals. Exotic animals were brought to the imperial zoo, and rare plants grew in the palace gardens.

THE CIVIL SERVICE
Officials held great power in governing China. Some worked in the capital. Others were placed in charge of provinces, which were divided into smaller districts and counties, with lesser officials in charge.

To become an official, a young man had first to pass examinations, held every three years. Candidates who passed local exams went on to provincial and then to national exams. All candidates had to show

that they knew the works of Confucius thoroughly. This meant learning all of the five classic books by heart.

The exams were held inside special compounds, shut off from the outside world to prevent cheating. Soldiers watched over the candidates, and were rewarded with silver if they caught anyone cheating. The candidates spent two days as virtual prisoners in cramped cells, scribbling away with brush and ink, and listening to the sighs of their neighbors.

Passing the examinations did not guarantee a job. A successful candidate still needed to win the support of a senior official, on whom his career would depend. In the late 15th century, there were only 100,000 imperial civil servants in the whole of China. For every new successful candidate appointed, as many as 3,000 others went home disappointed.

Detail from a 17th-century painting showing Han Emperor Siuen Li with scholars translating classical texts.

All government officials had to pass rigorous examinations. This 18th-century painting shows candidates taking the examination to become country magistrates (judges).

Sometimes the emperor went on a grand tour to visit parts of his empire. This painting shows the vast procession attending the emperor Kangzi during such a journey in 1699. Kangzi was regarded as a model ruler, a student of Confucius, and a respecter of China's ancient traditions.

Chinese teaching urged people to seek explanations. The Chinese excelled in science and their many inventions include the umbrella, wheelbarrow, kite, abacus, paper, and gunpowder. They used waterwheels to drive mills and heavy hammers. Some inventions, like the compass, were soon copied in the West.

Panning for tin in a stream. Chinese miners also dug for coal and drilled for underground salt and natural gas.

TECHNOLOGY

Although they had an enormous supply of human labor, the Chinese were quick to adapt good ideas for making work simpler and faster. Transportation inventions included an improved horse harness, the breast strap, which did not choke the horse as the older neck harness often did. They also invented the wheelbarrow. Wheelbarrows were used in China from the fourth century A.D. Some were even fitted with sails.

METALS AND MACHINES

The Chinese had worked with bronze since Shang times. Chinese metalworkers progressed to making cast and wrought (beaten) iron and steel by A.D. 600.

In the Tang and Song dynasties, water power was used to drive hammers (for forging metal) or to mill rice. Waterwheels also drove textile machines with highly complicated arrangements of crankwheels, toothed cogs, and piston rods.

A drawing from the 17th century showing how silk is made. Women reared the silkworms, drew off the silk, and did the dyeing and weaving. The Chinese believed that silkworms were afraid of strangers, and warned them if visitors were expected.

The educated believe nothing, the uneducated believe everything.

———— *Chinese proverb* ————

GOVERNMENT AND SCIENCE

The distinction between science and magic was not always clear, but in general the government supported experimentation. Chang Heng (A.D. 78–139) was a mathematician and astronomer, as well as a civil servant. He worked out an accurate approximation of pi (π) for measuring circles, used the grid system in mapmaking, and made a seismograph to indicate the direction to an earthquake.

Europe before the 12th century A.D. Chinese ships were particularly seaworthy. Inside the hull were a number of watertight compartments so that the ship did not sink easily, even if holed.

In the 12th century A.D., the Song navy used paddleboats. These man-powered riverboats had 11 wheels on each side and another at the stern. They were armed with catapults to hurl gunpowder bombs.

WAR AND WEAPONS

The Chinese not only had the best crossbows, but terrifying fire weapons—flamethrowers, smokescreens, and gunpowder. Rockets were used for entertainment as well as war from the 10th century A.D. By the 17th century, armies had rocket batteries mounted on wheelbarrows.

PAPER

The invention of paper, one of the most important of all Chinese innovations, was announced in A.D. 105. Printing on paper began about 500 years later. The Chinese were the first to use paper money.

An earthquake indicator. If the ground shook, a pendulum moved, causing one of the dragons to release a ball that fell into the mouth of one of the pointer-frogs beneath.

This 19th-century painting shows a Chinese doctor taking a patient's pulse. Chinese medicine was based on the ideas of yin and yang. Doctors used acupuncture, or needle treatment, to release excess yin or yang from 365 points on the body.

This is an astronomical clock made by Sa Sun at Kaifeng in 1092. Moving wheels and spheres showed the changing positions of the stars and planets.

CLOCKS

To measure time, the Chinese used water clocks or sundials, or burned marked incense sticks. They also made bamboo springs for clocks, like the large astronomical clock shown in the picture, which was water-driven and had a gong to strike the hours.

THE SEA AND SHIPS

The Chinese made the first magnetic compasses. They took a naturally magnetic lodestone, and fixed to it a wooden fish, so it would float on water. A needle on the fish pointed south.

At sea, Chinese ships were steered by stern rudders, which worked better than steering oars. Rudders were used from the first century B.C., but did not appear in

此中國醫道之圖也京中醫士有太醫御醫之稱乃是在太醫院應差者如有人請馬錢醫二吊四百文四吊八百不等如來到門首看病者給錢數百名為門脉

During the Song dynasty China had reached new heights of brilliance in arts and the sciences. But in the 13th century a terrifying enemy swept into China from the north. Rockets and flamethrowers could not stop hordes of Mongol horsemen. The invaders took China by storm. The Song dynasty ended in 1279, and Mongol emperors sat on the imperial throne of China.

Mongol soldiers attack a walled city. They have set up ladders to climb the walls and built siege towers to reach the battlements. The Chinese fought stubbornly, but could not stop the waves of Mongol attacks.

> Their horses are so well trained for quick-change movements, that upon the signal given, they instantly turn in every direction; and by these rapid maneuvers, many victories have been obtained.
>
> ———————— *Marco Polo* ————————

THE MONGOLS

The Mongols were not farmers like the Chinese. Every Mongol man was a soldier. He rode and fought from boyhood. He preferred the wild plains to the well-ordered city.

The Mongols struck fear into all the peoples of Asia and west into Europe. To the Chinese, the Mongols were barbarians. They hoped the Great Wall would keep the enemy out, but it did not. The northern border states of Hsia and Kin were wiped out by Genghis Khan's armies. By 1220, the Mongols controlled much of northern China. They seemed unbeatable. Their armies invaded Russia and captured Baghdad (in Iraq) in 1258.

The Mongols were cavalry soldiers, who charged into battle on well-trained horses, firing arrows. But they quickly learned new methods of warfare. They became expert at sieges. When they mastered the use of new Chinese weapons such as rockets and cannons, they became even more formidable.

Mongol cavalry (right), from a Persian manuscript illustration. Chinese rebels hid messages inside cakes baked for the harvest festival. When Chinese families cut the cakes and read the message "Kill the Mongol," they fell upon their enemies.

38

Genghis Khan (1162–1227) was the greatest conqueror of the Middle Ages. This Persian painting shows him in his tent. His armies created the legend of the "Mongol fury." The emperor Kublai Khan (1216–1294) was his grandson.

an efficient service for letters, carried by fast riders. But the Mongols were not interested in China's farms and cities.

RUIN, RESENTMENT, REVOLT

The China that Marco Polo saw and thought so magnificent was a shadow of its old splendor. Wise advisors suggested to the Mongols that they govern China kindly. Then its people would again prosper and pay taxes. Other counselors urged the killing of all Chinese. The Yuan emperors remained hated foreign rulers.

By the mid-14th century, the Mongol war machine had run out of steam. In China, secret societies flourished and rebels attacked barges on the Grand Canal. In 1367, a monk-turned-bandit named Zhu Yuanzhuang led a revolt. The last Mongol ruler fled. The bandit made himself emperor, and took the name Ming Hong Wu.

The Ming dynasty ruled China from 1368 until 1644. It was during this period that the West began for the first time to intrude in Chinese affairs.

MONGOL CHINA

The last Song emperor died in 1279. By then China was ruled by the Mongol leader Kublai Khan, from his base at Beijing (Peking). The new Mongol rulers, the Yuan, controlled China until 1368.

Foreigners themselves, the Yuan rulers chose foreign officials to work for them. These included Marco Polo, who served Kublai Khan. The new rulers brought some benefits, including better roads and

The Chinese fought the Mongols with crossbows, like this one, carried by a soldier. There were also much bigger crossbows.

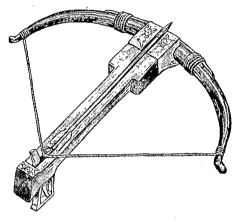

In 1421, the Ming emperor Yung Le decided to make the old Mongol city of Beijing his imperial capital. This northern city became the heart of China. Within its walls was the Forbidden City, the home of the emperor and his family. Few Chinese, and no foreigners, were allowed beyond its gates into the palaces and parks.

HOME FOR AN EMPEROR

The imperial home was a symbol of the supreme power of the emperor. A million workers toiled for ten years to build the Forbidden City. It was surrounded by a moat and inside were many walled courtyards. Within the walls, every terrace and gate faced south. The Meridian Gate was an awe-inspiring entrance, beyond which no foreigners were admitted.

This see-through scene shows an outer gateway to the Forbidden City, and beyond it the Gate of Supreme Harmony, the entrance to the emperor's throne room. China's finest artists helped to decorate the Forbidden City. Roof beams, handrails, arches, staircases, and stone animals were all crafted with enormous skill. Columns holding up roofs were covered with gold and entwined with carved dragons. Floors were made from gleaming white marble.

1 Side pavilion
2 Carved stone
  animals
3 Gate of Supreme
  Harmony
4 Wooden columns
5 Carved and
  painted wooden
  decoration
6 Courtyard wall of
  carved stone
7 Court officials
8 Side pavilion

THE EMPEROR'S SECRET WORLD

Beyond the gate was a huge paved courtyard with a river flowing across it. Five bridges crossed the river. In the huge Hall of Supreme Harmony, the emperor received visitors. Behind it were two other halls: one was a waiting room, the other a banquet hall. Nearby were sacrificial altars where the emperor prayed to Earth, Sun, and Moon.

The emperor and his family enjoyed private parks, gardens, lakes, pagodas, and pavilions. Some chosen scholars and officials lived and worked in the city, but the emperor lived in almost total seclusion, guarded by loyal eunuchs.

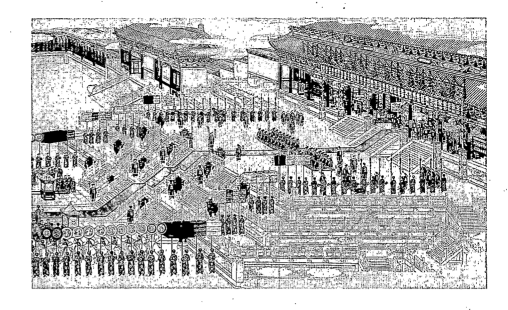

This picture shows imperial finery during the Qing or Manchu period (1644–1912). Officials, foot guards, and horsemen stand in impressive array on the steps of the Forbidden City. Within the great Hall of Supreme Harmony, the emperor sat on his dragon throne. The architecture of the palaces is among the most magnificent in all China. The buildings are huge, some over 300 feet long, and brightly colored, with red plastered bricks and yellow-painted timbers.

41

THE WORLD OUTSIDE

When European ships first sailed into China's ports, the Chinese treated the strangers warily—as curiosities or pirates. China wanted nothing from the West, but the West was determined to trade with China. Western merchants were eager to buy silks, porcelain, and tea. Later, they reinforced their demands with warships. As Western influence grew, imperial rule weakened.

Chinese porcelain, like this 18th-century Ming plate made for export, was greatly admired in Europe and America. Shiploads of pottery were brought from China, and Chinese styles were imitated by pottery factories in the West.

MING AND QING

Ming rule lasted until 1644, when invaders from Manchuria conquered China. The new Manchu, or Qing, dynasty was the last of China's great ruling families. The Qing emperors governed China in much the same way as the Ming.

WESTERN SHIPS AND POWER

For hundreds of years, all of China's invaders had come from the land. The Great Wall was still the empire's front line. Chinese overseas exploration stopped, and after 1551, it was illegal for any large Chinese ship to sail outside home waters.

China sought to cut itself off from the outside world. But the outside world was reaching toward China. In 1514, the first Portuguese ship arrived. Dutch and English traders followed. The Europeans set up trading stations. Few people in Europe knew much about China, and the traders made little effort to understand Chinese ways.

An official of the Dutch East India Company watches as chests of tea are loaded on board one of the trading company's ships. The Chinese did not want trade with the West, but were increasingly powerless to stop it.

CHINA AND THE FOREIGNERS

The greatest of the Qing emperors was Kangzi (1662–1722). His armies conquered Taiwan, Mongolia, and Tibet. China now seemed as powerful a nation as ever, but appearances were deceptive.

The Chinese government at first allowed Westerners to trade only through one port, Guangzhou. Unable to sell their factory goods in China, Westerners began selling opium, a drug banned by the Chinese government. This led to the Opium War of 1839. The ill-equipped Chinese were defeated. They were forced to open five ports to foreigners, and to hand over Hong Kong to Britain.

THE END OF THE EMPIRE

From 1851 to 1864, millions of Chinese died during a civil war, the Taiping Rebellion. China could not match the new industrial and military strength of foreign countries. By the end of the 19th century, Britain, Russia, France, Germany, and Japan had all managed to seize chunks of Chinese territory.

In 1900, there was a violent but unsuccessful uprising against foreigners in China known as the Boxer Rebellion. The Qing government tried to modernize China's schools and factories, but it was too late. In 1912 revolutionaries set up a republic, led by Sun Yat-sen. The empire was over.

CIVIL WAR AND COMMUNISM

A long and bitter civil war between Chinese Nationalists and Communists followed. In 1937, Japanese armies invaded China, adding to the destruction. Finally, in 1949, the Communists triumphed and their leader, Mao Zedong (Mao Tse-tung), took China into a new and unique age.

There have been many changes since: the "Cultural Revolution" of the 1960s, trends toward a Western-style economy, and the crushing of pro-democracy campaigns such as the Tiananmen Square massacre of the late 1980s.

This Chinese illustration, about 1850, shows tea being graded and weighed for packing. Tea was a popular drink in Britain from the 18th century. In the 19th century, fast-sailing ships called clippers carried tea from China to Europe.

A Chinese war junk is destroyed by fire from a British warship in 1841 during the Opium War. By the 19th century, the Chinese lagged behind the West in technology. The Industrial Revolution had given Europeans and Americans an edge over China.

These Chinese stamps show (top) a statue of Buddha, from Yungang Grotto; (middle) the sea goddess Mazu; and (bottom) a model of a traditional house from Fujian.

A charioteer and attendant officers, from the vast tomb army of the First Emperor. Every one of the terracotta soldiers is an individual, even though the army was created in a workshop that must have been like an assembly line. The detail of each figure has told historians a great deal about the clothing and equipment of Chinese soldiers.

After years of isolation under Communist rule, today China is open to tourists and trade. Visitors walk the Great Wall and admire the tomb treasures of the emperors. Modern science has uncovered long-lost wonders, and told us much more about how the people of ancient China lived.

OLD AND NEW TOGETHER

During the Cultural Revolution, which was encouraged in the 1960s by the Communist leader Mao Zedong, the Communists tried for a time to destroy old traditions, just as the First Emperor had tried to burn ancient books. But they did not succeed. In modern China, with its factories and fast-food restaurants, the old China still speaks powerfully, and ancient traditions live on.

LOST AND FOUND

The Chinese have uncovered much of their past by excavating the tombs of vanished dynasties. Before the 20th century and the end of the Chinese empire, no one was allowed to interfere with royal tombs. Serious study of the past began in the 1920s with the excavation by archaeologists of the Shang tombs in northwest China.

At the same time, scientists were finding the far older remains of "Peking Man"—the bones of early cave-dwelling people. This find sparked interest in prehistoric China. The bones were due to be shipped to America for safekeeping in 1939, but they disappeared. Where they went is one of the great unsolved mysteries of modern archaeology. What is certain is that "modern" human beings were living in China 25,000 years ago.

MODERN ARCHAEOLOGY

In the 1950s, scientists working near Beijing dug into the tomb of a Ming emperor—the first Ming tomb to be opened. Inside they found rare porcelain and rolls of silk, each marked with the date and place it was made. Such detail is typical of the painstaking care taken by the officials in charge of burying important people. From detailed examination of mummified bodies found in tombs, scientists have been able to tell much about how people lived in imperial China.

TALES OF THE TOMBS

The most amazing tomb find was the terracotta army buried with the First Emperor, Shi Huang. In 1979, peasants digging a well broke through into the burial mound where thousands of clay model soldiers were buried. Nothing like it is known anywhere else in the world.

Most finds are now made by teams of government scientists and scholars. Often the archaeologists open a tomb but find it empty. China has always had many tomb robbers, and today there is an illegal trade in ancient treasures. However, even an empty tomb can yield secrets: a 2,000-year-old tomb found in 1993 near Xian had a star map painted on the ceiling—which no tomb robbers could remove.

Chinese character for "By order of the emperor."

PRESERVING THE PAST

Archaeology is often a race against time, as the modern world threatens to destroy the heritage of the past. At present, China's government is removing many tombs, and their treasures, from the path of a huge new dam and reservoir project on the Chang Jiang (Yangtze River).

Exhibitions and displays of Chinese art and sculpture, including pieces recovered from ancient tombs, have toured the world. These have made people more aware of the beauty and variety of China's art. Chinese inventions have also become better known and taken up by Western technology. Tourists can visit the sites and museums in China to learn more about China and its brilliant past. What we know of the lives of ordinary Chinese people over so many centuries reveals an astonishing continuity.

The Chinese today are heirs to the world's oldest unbroken cultural tradition, a way of life that has lasted for more than five thousand years and continues to thrive.

China's history is one of continuity. The neon signs in this street are modern, but the language and the traditions that have shaped the people who live and work there are ancient.

This book can only touch on some of the events and achievements of China in the past 5,000 years. Listed below are the main dynastic periods, with some of their achievements and important events.

Early Times: to 1122 B.C.
Over 500,000 years ago: Stone Age hunters and gatherers
3000 B.C.: First villages and farmers
2200 B.C.: Legendary dynasty of Hsia
1500 B.C.: Shang. Bronze-working

First Empires: 1122 B.C. to A.D. 618
1122 B.C.: Zhou dynasty, followed by Spring and Autumn and Warring States periods (770–221 B.C.)
500 B.C. Confucius, Lao-tzu. First Emperor Shi Huang-di
202 B.C. to A.D. 220: Han Empire. Trade with Europe begins
220–581: Three kingdoms and six dynasties run their courses, and Buddhism arrives in China
581–618: Sui dynasty. Grand Canal

The Great Dynasties: A.D. 618 to 1368
618–907: Tang dynasty brings prosperity and advances in arts and technology
907–960: Five dynasties and ten kingdoms period—brief military dictatorships. Porcelain and printing
960: China reunified by Song general Chao Kuang-yin
960–1126: Northern Song. Conquered by Kin nomads
1127–1279: Southern Song. Golden age of painting and philosophy. Mongol attacks begin
1279: Song dynasty ends
1260–1294: Reign of Kublai Khan
1271–1297: Marco Polo in China
1279–1368: Mongol conquest and Yuan Empire

This picture of the emperor Kangzi's tour of Kiang-Han captures an essential element of China's art and thought. The landscape is calm and ordered. Trees, rocks, and river provide an eternal background to human activity.

Ming and Qin dynasties: 1368–1912

1368–1644: Ming Dynasty. Beijing becomes China's capital. The Forbidden City. Chinese ships make voyages to India, the Middle East, Indonesia, and Africa. First European sailors arrive (Portuguese in 1514, Dutch in 1622, British in 1637)

1644–1912: Manchu, or Qing Dynasty

1839–1842: Opium War

1851–1864: Taiping Rebellion

1900: Boxer Rebellion (against foreigners)

1949: Communism. Mao Zedong (Mao Tse-tung)

1989: Tiananmen Square massacre

GLOSSARY

archaeologist: person who studies the life and culture of ancient peoples

barbarian: uncivilized person; the Chinese thought most foreigners were barbarians

Buddhism: teachings of Buddha (about 563–483 B.C.); originated in India

cavalry: soldiers fighting on horseback

civil servant: government official, trained to serve the emperor

crossbow: weapon that fires an arrow when the bowstring is wound back and then released by a trigger

dynasty: a line of several rulers belonging to the same family

eunuch: castrated male servant

jade: hard stone used for carving and jewelry, usually white or green

lacquer: varnish made from tree sap, used to give a polished look to wood

loess: fine yellow soil

noble, or **lord:** a landowner who had to fight for the emperor in return for his land

peasant: poor farmer who worked for a lord, but could own some land himself

shaman: person believed to be able to see into the future and tell fortunes

tomb: burial place, often underground

QUOTATIONS

The *Shiji* was a book written about 210 B.C. based on the writings of the scholar Li Si. King Pan Geng was the Shang ruler who, in 1400 B.C., moved his court to Anyang. Marco Polo (1254–1342), a Venetian, spent 17 years in China, and gave Europeans their first glimpse of life in China. Lao-tzu was one of the greatest philosophers of China. He probably lived in the sixth century B.C. Xunzi (340–245 B.C.) was a philosopher who worked at an academy in the state of Qi.

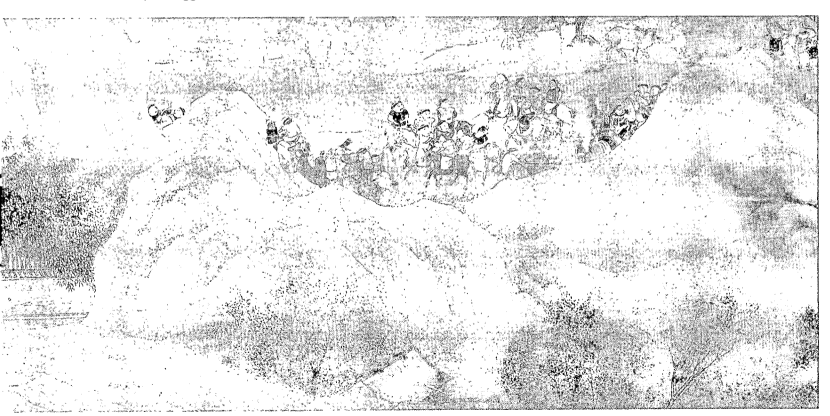

47

INDEX